A once-mighty emperor
stands before his captor,
begging for his life.

The Emperor

The emperor is Atahualpa. He ruled over millions of people in the vast Inca Empire. The empire sprawls for thousands of miles along the west coast of South America.

The Captor

The captor is Francisco Pizarro, a 61-year-old soldier from Spain. For 20 years he has battled his way across South America in search of glory, land, and gold. The riches he seeks are finally within reach.

Showdown

More than 100,000 Inca warriors are loyal to Atahualpa. Pizarro has just 200 Spanish soldiers. But the Spaniards are heavily armed and hungry for treasure. They are determined to make the Inca Empire their prize.

The Question

How could 200 soldiers hope to conquer an empire of millions of people? What motivated conquistadors like Pizarro to destroy civilizations?

PREVIEW PHOTOS

PAGE 1: Pizarro (with sword) threatens Inca ruler Atahualpa.

PAGES 2–3: Atahualpa (with feathered headdress) tries to negotiate with Pizarro.

PAGES 4–5: Pizarro's men attack the Incas at the Battle of Cajamarca.

Book Design: Red Herring Design/NYC **Photo Credits:** Photographs © 2012: Alamy Images: 31 top right (Steve Allen Travel Photography), 30 top (John Mitchell); Art Resource, NY: 17 (bpk, Berlin/Ethnologisches Museum, Staatliche Museen, Berlin/Dietrich Graf), 44 center (Amable-Paul Coutan/Reunion des Musees Nationaux/Franck Raux), 14, 16, 27, 38 (Theodore de Bry/bpk, Berlin/Kunstbibliothek, Staatliche Museen, Berlin/Knud Petersen), 20, 21 (The New York Public Library); Bridgeman Art Library International Ltd., London/New York: 45 center left (Brooklyn Museum of Art, New York), 45 top right (from *Narrative and Critical History of America*, pub. 1889/Private Collection), 41 (Poma de Ayala, Felipe Huaman/Biblioteca del ICI, Madrid/Index), 29 (Private Collection/Archives Charmet); Corbis Images: 32 (Bettmann), 44 bottom left (D.K. Bonatti/Philip de Bay/Historical Picture Archive), 43 (Antonio de Herrara/Brooklyn Museum), 44 bottom right (Gallo Gallina/Philip de Bay/Historical Picture Archive), 22, 23 (Bob Krist), 4, 5 (Herbert Tauss/National Geographic Society); Getty Images/Michael Langford: 31 top left; Mark Summers: cover; Military and Historical Image Bank/www.historicalimagebank.com: 30 center right; NEWSCOM: 2, 3 (Album/Kurwenal/Prisma), 45 center right (Album/Mestral/Prisma), 30 center left (Album/Oronoz), 42 (Oronoz); North Wind Picture Archives: 18, 24, 37; Peabody Museum of Archaeology and Ethnology, Harvard University/No. 39-83-30/1870: 31 bottom right; ShutterStock, Inc./Michael Drager: back cover; Superstock, Inc./age fotostock: 31 center; The Art Archive/Picture Desk: 1 (Pierre-Nolasque Bergeret/Musee du Nouveau Monde La Rochelle/Gianni Dagli Orti), 31 bottom left (Biblioteca Nacional Madrid/Gianni Dagli Orti), 30 bottom; The Granger Collection, New York: 8, 13, 34 bottom, 35 bottom, 44 top left, 44 top right, 45 top left; The Image Works: 44 top center (akg-images), 30 center (akg-images/Interfoto), 45 bottom (J. Bedmar/Iberfoto), 10 (CAGP/Iberfoto), 34 top (Topham).

With thanks to Karen Baicker

Library of Congress Cataloging-in-Publication Data
Jacobs, Lucy.
Conquistador : Francisco Pizarro ravages the Inca Empire / Lucy Jacobs.
p. cm. — (Xbooks)
Includes bibliographical references and index.
ISBN-13: 978-0-545-32940-8
ISBN-10: 0-545-32940-X
1. Pizarro, Francisco, ca. 1475-1541—Juvenile literature.
2. Peru—History—Conquest, 1522-1548—Juvenile literature.
3. Incas—Juvenile literature. 4. Governors—Peru—Biography—Juvenile literature. 5. Explorers—Peru—Biography—Juvenile literature.
6. Explorers—Spain—Biography—Juvenile literature. I. Title.
F3442.P776J32 2012
985'.02092—dc23
[B]
2011023333

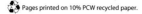 Pages printed on 10% PCW recycled paper.

3 4 5 6 7 8 9 10   40   21 20 19 18 17 16 15 14

CONQUISTADOR

Francisco Pizarro
Ravages the Inca Empire

LUCY JACOBS

FRANCISCO PIZARRO INVADED the Inca Empire in 1532. His mission was simple. "I came here to take away their gold," he said.

TABLE OF CONTENTS

1

Back to America

An old warrior wants one more chance at fame and fortune.

Francisco Pizarro had to fight for everything he gained in life. He was born in the Spanish province of Extremadura, a name that means "remote and harsh." As a teenager, Pizarro worked as a pig farmer. Then he joined the army in search of wealth and adventure.

Now, in the summer of 1528, he stood before King Charles V of Spain. Pizarro had spent 20 years exploring and conquering land in the Americas. He had been with the first Europeans when they reached the eastern edge of the Pacific Ocean. He had ruled the city of Panama, the most important Spanish colony in the New World.

Greedy for Gold

But Pizarro wanted the king's blessing for one more mission. South of Panama lay a vast continent that was still largely unexplored by Europeans. The Spanish called the western part of this unknown land "Peru." It was ruled by an emperor rumored to possess a huge fortune in gold. Pizarro wanted that fortune for Spain—and for himself.

King Charles offered Pizarro a deal. The conquistador, or conqueror, would travel to South America with a small army of recruits. If Pizarro conquered Peru, he would govern the new colony and control its wealth. In exchange, Pizarro would send one-fifth of his treasure back to the king.

In the spring of 1530, Pizarro and his crew—including three of his half brothers, Hernando, Juan, and Gonzalo—arrived in Panama. There they rejoined

Pizarro's former partner Diego de Almagro. Like Pizarro, Almagro was a fierce conquistador. He had lost an eye during a battle with Indians on the South American coast.

Almagro was angry to discover that he was barely mentioned in the king's agreement with Pizarro. After some arguing, Pizarro finally agreed to split any territory they conquered. But neither man walked away satisfied. The tension in their partnership would come back to haunt them both.

PIZARRO TOOK JUST 180 SOLDIERS to Peru. One soldier wrote, "When has so great an enterprise been undertaken by so few against so many odds . . . to conquer the unknown?"

2

A Rough Start

Pizarro and his men struggle
through the jungle in heavy armor.

On December 27, 1530, Pizarro sailed south from
Panama to Peru. He took just three ships, 180 men,
and 27 horses. The journey tested even the most
rugged men in Pizarro's party. In March 1531, storms
forced the ships ashore on the northern edge of the
Inca Empire. The empire stretched more than
2,000 miles down the coast. The Spaniards continued
southward by land.

PIZARRO'S MEN make landfall in Tumbes.

By the fall, Pizarro's men were exhausted. Their progress was slow. Many Spaniards had been killed by starvation and disease. Then, in December, a conquistador named Hernando de Soto arrived to join the expedition. He brought 100 men, more horses, and a couple of ships. Pizarro made de Soto a captain. Together, they settled in to wait out the winter rains.

HUASCAR (right) and his half brother Atahualpa fought for control of the Inca Empire. The fighting began after an outbreak of smallpox killed 200,000 Incas, including their father, Emperor Huayna Capac.

A Divided Empire

In the spring of 1532, Pizarro sailed to Tumbes, a gold-rich coastline 1,000 miles south of Panama. He had been there before, during an earlier attempt to find Peru. Pizarro had found the people both welcoming and wealthy.

But this time, Pizarro was shocked by what he found. The village lay in ruins. Homes had been looted and destroyed. Crops were burned. The ground was littered with corpses.

The few survivors told Pizarro that the empire was being torn apart by civil war. Two half brothers, Atahualpa and Huascar, were battling for power. More than 100,000 Incas had been killed.

This was good news to Pizarro. The war had left the empire divided and weak. He could not have timed his expedition better.

MOVING SOUTH, the Spaniards crossed treacherous mountains. As they inched forward along narrow ledges, giant condors flew by, sending startled men tumbling to their deaths.

3

No Turning Back

Atahualpa watches as the Spaniards approach the Inca war camp.

In the summer of 1532, Pizarro and his men marched south under the watching eyes of Atahualpa's scouts. The Spaniards were headed toward the emperor's war camp at Cajamarca. But for the ruler of millions, a band of 200 starving men wasn't alarming.

And Atahualpa had a more pressing concern. He had just defeated his half brother Huascar in battle— and slaughtered his family. Still, thousands of Huascar's

PIZARRO POINTS to the city of Cajamarca, where Emperor Atahualpa was waiting with 50,000 warriors.

followers had survived. And they were seething over their leader's murder. They must have seemed far more dangerous to Atahualpa than Pizarro's ragged party.

Advance on Atahualpa

But Pizarro and his men were more of a threat than they appeared. Their weapons superior to the Incas', and the Spanish army was gaining strength. As the conquistadors marched, they pressured local tribes to join them. Many rulers were hostile to Atahualpa and eager to help. Those who resisted were treated brutally.

Finally, after several days in the mountains, Pizarro and his men looked out over the valley of Cajamarca. Stretching before them was a huge city of stone and brick houses. It was larger than any city in Spain. Towering over one corner of the city was a giant temple to the Inca sun god. Beyond it lay a fearsome sight: the Inca army's campsite. There were two miles of tents for more than 50,000 warriors. "The spectacle caused … fear in the stoutest heart," wrote one Spanish soldier. "But it was too late to turn back."

Mighty Empire

Here are some FAQs about the Inca Empire, one of the greatest civilizations of all time.

HOW BIG WAS THE INCA EMPIRE?

Enormous! It stretched for 2,500 miles and included several large cities. The Incas referred to it as Tawantinsuyu, or "the four quarters of the world."

No one knows exactly how many people lived under Inca rule. Estimates range from four million to 37 million.

WHO WERE THE INCAS?

At first the Incas were one tribe among many on the western coast of South America. They built the city of Cuzco around the year 1200. From there they slowly expanded their influence over tribes to the north and south. Tribes that resisted were conquered, and their leaders were executed.

THE RUINS of Machu Picchu sit high in the Andes mountains.

HOW ADVANCED WERE THE INCAS?

Incredibly advanced! They built some of the world's earliest suspension bridges. Made from vines and reeds, these bridges stretched across ravines in the mountains.

The Incas built thousands of miles of roads to connect villages. And their houses were architectural marvels, with stones carved to fit perfectly together.

HOW MUCH GOLD DID THEY HAVE?

Tons! Clothes were stitched with gold thread. The elite ate from gold plates and drank from gold cups. The emperor sat on a gold throne. Life-sized gold statues decorated the cities.

HAS ANY OF THE INCA EMPIRE SURVIVED?

The Spanish destroyed most of the Inca Empire. But the city of Machu Picchu remained hidden high in the clouds of the Andes mountains.

Archeologist Hiram Bingham found the city in 1911. There were palaces, tombs, and grand temples built from enormous stones. The buildings were so precisely constructed that a knife blade could not fit between the huge stones.

There were aqueducts that carried water to crops, and an observatory for studying the sky.

Today, Machu Picchu is one of the only remaining relics of the great Inca Empire.

FRIAR VICENTE VALVERDE (holding cross) speaks to Atahualpa, the Inca emperor.

4

Battle of Cajamarca

The Spaniards set a trap.

On November 15, 1532, Pizarro, de Soto, and the rest of the Spaniards descended into Cajamarca. One of Atahualpa's messengers welcomed them and promised that they would be treated well. Pizarro was wary. He had seen the signs of violence in Tumbes and other villages.

But de Soto was eager to visit Atahualpa. Pizarro agreed to send him to meet the emperor. De Soto chose five horsemen and a priest named Friar Vicente Valverde to go with him.

The tiny group donned their armor and rode to the great Inca camp outside the walls of Cajamarca. They passed rows of armed warriors and approached the emperor. "Hernando de Soto rode right up to him," Friar Vicente recalled, "and so close to him was he that his horse's nose touched his headdress."

The Inca warriors had never seen a horse before. Several of them stepped back in fear. But Atahualpa stood firm. When de Soto offered him a ring, he accepted the gift. According to Friar Vicente, Atahualpa would later execute more than 300 Incas for showing their fear of the horses.

A Deadly Invitation

A few days later, Pizarro sent his brother Hernando to visit Atahualpa. Over goblets of wine, Hernando invited Atahualpa to visit Pizarro in Cajamarca. Atahualpa accepted. Little did he know that the invitation was a trap.

The next day, Pizarro's secretary, Xeres, watched as Atahualpa arrived. "It was as if the entire valley was in movement," Xeres wrote. Thousands of men accompanied the emperor. They were mostly unarmed.

Atahualpa approached on a litter, a chair carried on the shoulders of his nobles. "Six hundred Indians . . . as if pieces of a chessboard came ahead of him," the secretary wrote. They swept stones off the road to clear the way for the emperor.

ATAHUALPA IS CARRIED on a litter to meet Francisco Pizarro.

Atahualpa's men crowded into Cajamarca's central square. But there was no one there to greet them. "What has become of the bearded ones?" Atahualpa asked his generals.

Setting a Trap

Just then, Friar Vicente appeared. He explained that the Spaniards would befriend Atahualpa, but only if the emperor converted to Christianity. Friar Vicente held up a prayer book. He said it contained the words of God. He told Atahualpa that their mission was to teach those words to the Incas.

Atahualpa held the mysterious object up to his ear, listening for words. Hearing none, he threw the book to the ground. That was all the excuse the Spaniards needed. Friar Vicente cried out, "At them! At them!"

At the signal, Pizarro's soldiers leaped from their hiding places. "The guns were fired off," Xeres recalled. "The trumpets sounded and the troops, both horse and foot, sallied forth."

The battle lasted just over half an hour. The Spaniards attacked with swords, lances, crossbows, and long guns called harquebuses. Many of the Inca warriors fled, but the horsemen chased them down. With fewer than 200 soldiers, the Spaniards slaughtered thousands of the Incas.

Atahualpa, however, was worth more to Pizarro alive than dead. "Let no one who values his life strike him," the conquistador shouted. He pulled Atahualpa by his hair, dragging him off his golden litter. The most powerful ruler in South America had been captured. And not a single Spanish soldier had been killed.

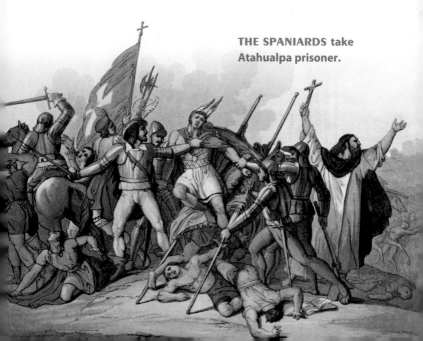

THE SPANIARDS take Atahualpa prisoner.

Armed &

The conquistadors were few in number, but they were armed to the teeth.

CONQUISTADORS

ARMOR: These suits of steel were built with hinges to allow movement. Underneath the armor, some soldiers wore chain mail.

HARQUEBUS: These three- to five-foot-long guns fired lead balls.

FALCONET: A small cannon

CROSSBOW AND BOLT: Crossbows fired steel-tipped bolts that flew with deadly force.

SWORDS: Spanish swords were made from the world's best steel. Flexible and sharp, they could behead a person with one expert blow.

Dangerous

Inca warriors outnumbered the Spaniards. But their weapons were no match for the conquistadors'.

INCA WARRIORS

SPIKED CLUB:
These heavy wood clubs were used in hand-to-hand combat.

SLINGSHOT: With a flick of the wrist, a stone could be launched from the cord with great speed and accuracy.

BOLAS: These ropes with weights at both ends were thrown to wrap around an enemy's legs.

JAVELIN: Spears were thrown or thrust at the enemy.

SPEARHEAD:
This heavy spiked spearhead was attached to the end of a wooden club.

31

PIZARRO (with long beard) orders his soldiers to take Emperor Atahualpa prisoner.

5

A Desperate Bargain

Atahualpa offers a roomful of
gold in exchange for his life.

On his first night as a prisoner, Atahualpa dined
with Pizarro. They ate in a large hall overlooking
Cajamarca's central square. The bodies of 2,000 Inca
warriors still littered the ground below them.

At night guards chained Atahualpa inside a house.
But Pizarro ordered his men to treat the emperor with
respect. Atahualpa's wives and servants were allowed
to stay with him. He continued to eat from gold plates.

Pizarro had severely weakened the Inca Empire in one brutal stroke. Seeing their leader humiliated, Atahualpa's warriors had deserted Cajamarca. The emperor still had 100,000 loyal soldiers within a week's march of the city. But word of his defeat spread quickly. One by one, village leaders came to pledge their loyalty to Pizarro.

ATAHUALPA OFFERED PIZARRO rooms full of gold and silver in exchange for his freedom.

An Emperor's Ransom

Not long after the battle, Pizarro visited Atahualpa in his jail cell. In exchange for his life, the emperor offered the Spaniards the one thing they truly wanted: gold. Atahualpa said his men would fill one room with gold and two more with silver. He lifted his arm above his head to show how high the treasure would be piled.

Pizarro immediately agreed. Atahualpa sent

orders to his people. Soon Inca lords began arriving in Cajamarca with the treasures of their civilization.

While waiting for the ransom, Pizarro and de Soto grew to respect their captive. De Soto taught the emperor to play chess. Hernando Pizarro taught Atahualpa to speak Spanish. As one Spaniard wrote, they were "astounded to find so much wisdom in a barbarian."

Looting an Empire

The ransom was paid by the summer of 1533. Three rooms were filled with gold and silver statues, shields, goblets, and jewelry. Pizarro ordered that every piece be thrown into red-hot fires and melted down. Inca goldsmiths spent months destroying the treasures of their empire. When they finished, Pizarro counted 13,000 pounds of gold bars and twice that amount in silver. As agreed, one-fifth of the riches were sent back to King Charles. The rest were divided among Pizarro and his men.

INCA ARTISTS created beautiful objects from gold, such as this llama. The Spaniards melted thousands of these treasures into gold bars.

Betrayal

In April 1533, Pizarro's partner and rival, Almagro, had arrived in Cajamarca with 150 men. He insisted that Atahualpa be executed—despite Pizarro's agreement with the emperor. If Atahualpa went free, Almagro argued, he might rally his troops against the Spaniards. Pizarro hesitated. What if the Incas tried to avenge the death of their emperor?

Pizarro made his decision. On the evening of July 26, Atahualpa was shackled. He was led to the torch-lit city square. Guards tied his neck to a stake. "Why are you going to kill me?" he cried out to his captors. "What have I or my sons or my wives ever done to you?" The emperor's servants and wives watched from inside his cell. They wailed and banged on the stone walls.

Pizarro was unmoved. He gave a signal. The rope tied around Atahualpa's neck was quickly tightened. His head snapped to one side, and the emperor was dead. The lifeless body of the last great Inca ruler was left in the city square. His wives and servants wept through the night.

ATAHUALPA PREPARES to be executed. Just before he was killed, the emperor agreed to convert to Christianity. In return the Spanish strangled him instead of burning him alive.

PIZARRO AND HIS ARMY of thousands approach Cuzco, the Inca capital.

6

New Regime

The Spaniards discover that ruling Peru isn't easy.

Atahualpa was dead. Control of his empire—and all its riches—lay within Pizarro's grasp.

Pizarro moved quickly to attack Cuzco, the Inca capital. His army now included thousands of Inca warriors. It took nearly a full day for the entire force to leave Cajamarca.

When Pizarro's army arrived in Cuzco on November 15, 1533, they met no resistance. Atahualpa's army had fled the grand city. Within hours, Pizarro's men were drunk. They looted Cuzco's palaces and temples. They dug up graves and stole jewelry from the dead. The Spaniards "are not the sons of God," an Inca lord complained, "but the sons of the Devil."

In the following months, Pizarro extended his control over the Inca Empire from his new headquarters in Cuzco. He granted land to wealthy Spanish settlers. He gave these Spanish landowners permission to use the Indians as laborers or soldiers. Under the law of their conquerors, the Incas had become virtual slaves.

A New Civil War

Near the end of 1534, Pizarro left Cuzco for the coast. Soon his half brothers were competing with Diego de Almagro for control of the city. Within two years, the struggle had erupted into war.

In 1538, Hernando Pizarro defeated Almagro on a battlefield near Cuzco. Hernando had the one-eyed conquistador chained to a stake and strangled. Almagro's head was cut off and stuck on the end of a lance, his one good eye still open.

THIS ILLUSTRATION from the
1500s shows Pizarro's brother
Gonzalo capturing Almagro.

Almagro's followers did not forget how Pizarro's men had killed their leader. Three years later, they stormed into Francisco Pizarro's palace. Pizarro, now nearly 70 years old, struggled to put on his armor. He slashed at his attackers, killing three of them. But as he was trying to free his sword from a body, the assassins sliced his throat with a knife.

Pizarro lay on the ground gasping for breath. Legend has it he drew a cross in a pool of his own blood. Seconds later, the conquistador was dead. ✘

PIZARRO DRAWS A CROSS with his blood as he lies dying.

X FILES

Timeline: The Conquistadors

1200:
The Inca Empire begins around this time in Peru.

1513: Pizarro travels to Panama with Vasco de Balboa, who becomes the first European to see the eastern edge of the Pacific Ocean.

1524: Pizarro and Diego de Almagro lead their first expedition to Peru.

1200	1471	1492	1513	1519	1524

c. 1471: Francisco Pizarro is born in Trujillo, Spain.

1519: Hernán Cortés conquers the Aztecs in Mexico.

1492: Christopher Columbus sails to the Americas on behalf of Spain.

1532: Pizarro defeats Inca emperor Atahualpa at Cajamarca.

1536-37: Spaniards put down a rebellion led by the Inca emperor Manco.

1538: Pizarro and his brothers defeat Almagro and execute him.

525-27   1528   1532 1533   1536-37 1538   1541

1528: Pizarro gets permission from King Charles V of Spain to lead an expedition to Peru.

1541: Pizarro is assassinated in Lima, Peru.

1533: Atahualpa is executed. Pizarro captures Cuzco, the Inca capital.

1525-27: Inca emperor Huayna Capac dies, and civil war breaks out between his successors.

RESOURCES

HERE'S A SELECTION of books and websites for more information about Francisco Pizarro and the Incas.

What to Read Next

NONFICTION

Calvert, Patricia. *The Ancient Inca* (People of the Ancient World). New York: Franklin Watts, 2005.

DiConsiglio, John. *Francisco Pizarro: Destroyer of the Inca Empire*. New York: Franklin Watts, 2009.

Gruber, Beth. *National Geographic Investigates: Ancient Inca: Archaeology Unlocks the Secrets of the Inca's Past*. Washington, DC: National Geographic Children's Books, 2007.

Kops, Deborah. *Machu Picchu* (Unearthing Ancient Worlds). Minneapolis: Twenty-First Century Books, 2009.

Somervill, Barbara. *Francisco Pizarro: Conqueror of the Incas*. Minneapolis: Compass Point Books, 2005.

Sonneborn, Liz. *Pizarro: Conqueror of the Mighty Incas*. Berkeley Heights, NJ: Enslow Publishers, 2010.

FICTION

Kerr, P. B. *The Eye of the Forest*. New York: Orchard Books, 2009.

O'Dell, Scott. *The Seven Serpents Trilogy*. Naperville, IL: Sourcebooks Jabberwocky, 2009.

Websites

Inca Mummies: Secrets of a Lost World
www.nationalgeographic.com/inca

National Geographic created this companion site for its fascinating series *Inca Mummies: Secrets of a Lost World*. It includes an online documentary.

Conquistadors
www.pbs.org/conquistadors

This companion site to the PBS series *Conquistadors* includes a section on the episode "Francisco Pizarro: The Conquest of the Incas."

Ghosts of Machu Picchu
www.pbs.org/wgbh/nova/ancient/ghosts-machu-picchu.html

Explore the mystery of why the Incas abandoned their magnificent city in the clouds, and find out more about Inca weapons and technology.

ASSASSIN (uh-SASS-uhn) *noun* a murderer of an important person

CAPTOR (KAP-tur) *noun* someone who takes and holds a person by force

CHAIN MAIL (CHAYN MAYL) *noun* flexible armor made of interlinked metal rings

CIVILIZATION (siv-i-luh-ZAY-shuhn) *noun* a highly developed and organized society

CONDOR (KON-dur) *noun* a large vulture

CONQUER (KONG-kur) *verb* to defeat and take control of an enemy

CONQUISTADOR (kuhn-KEES-ta-door) *noun* a Spanish warrior who took part in the conquest of the Americas

CORPSE (KORPS) *noun* a dead body

EMPEROR (EM-pur-ur) *noun* the male ruler of an empire

EMPIRE (EM-pire) *noun* a group of regions that have the same ruler

EXECUTE (EK-suh-kyoot) *verb* to kill as a punishment for a crime

EXPEDITION (ek-spuh-DISH-uhn) *noun* a long journey for a special purpose, such as exploring

GOBLET (GOB-lit) *noun* a tall drinking glass with a stem and a base

LANCE (LANSS) *noun* a long spear

LOOT (LOOT) *verb* to steal things during a riot or a war

RANSOM (RAN-suhm) *noun* money or valuables demanded for the release of a prisoner

RECOIL (ree-KOIL) *verb* to pull back in fear, horror, or disgust

RECRUIT (ri-KROOT) *noun* someone who has just joined a group

RIVAL (RYE-vuhl) *noun* an opponent or competitor

SEETHE (SEETH) *verb* to be filled with intense anger

SHACKLE (SHAK-uhl) *verb* to lock metal rings around the wrists or ankles of a prisoner

SUSPENSION BRIDGE (suh-SPEN-shuhn BRIJ) *noun* a bridge with a deck supported by and hung from ropes or cables

TREACHEROUS (TRECH-ur-uhss) *adjective* dangerous

VIRTUAL (VUR-choo-uhl) *adjective* almost, nearly

INDEX

METRIC CONVERSIONS

Feet to meters: 1 ft is about 0.3 m
Miles to kilometers: 1 mi is about 1.6 km
Pounds to kilograms: 1 lb is about 0.45 kg